Vegetaria

Cookbo

Thai Food made simple with over 77 recipes for amazing veggie dishes

Adele Tyler

All trademarks and brands within this book are for clarifying purposes only and are owned by the owners themselves, not affiliated with this document.

Contents

CHAPTER 3: VEGGIE THAI DINNER RECIPES 58

CHAPTER 4: VEGGIE THAI SNACK RECIPES.........83

Introduction

Thailand is the most acclaimed country in the whole world for its cooking. Exploring the southern landmass toward the northern regions, the nation offers an alternate mix of wildly scrumptious food. The south of Thailand is acclaimed for its intensely hot curries, significant coconut milk utilization, and amazing fish plans.

The northeastern part is amazing for its filled plates of mixed green vegetables, flame broiled meat, frankfurters, and relentless rice. Bangkok, the best city, draws in Thais from all over the nation to make a never-ending blend of appealing flavors to taste.

From streak cooked sautés to hand beaten servings of blended greens, on the off chance that you value eating, you will be in paradise with the collection and measure of food in this cooking given in this book. You will get more than 77 diverse vegetarian breakfast, vegetarian lunch, vegetarian snack, and vegetarian dinner plans that you can undoubtedly begin cooking at home with the detailed guidelines present beneath every recipe.

Setting up your simple Thai food at home, without the need to arrange food from some eateries, can turn out to be exceptionally simple once you begin perusing this book. Anyway, why sit tight and wait? Allow yourself to dive into the universe of Thai food.

Chapter 1: The World of Veggie Thai Breakfast Recipes

In this chapter, you will learn some amazing Thai vegetarian breakfast dishes that you can easily make at home on your own.

1.1 Wok Tofu Omelet Recipe

Preparation time: 15 minutes

Cooking Time: 10 minutes

Serving: 2

Ingredients:

- Green onions, two
- Sesame oil, two teaspoon
- Fried shallots, two tablespoon
- Beans sprouts, half cup
- Sweet chili sauce, one tablespoon
- Soy sauce, two tablespoon
- Peanut oil, two tablespoon
- Salt to taste
- Black pepper to taste
- Tofu, two cups
- Eggs, four

Instructions:

1. In a small container, whisk together all fixings well.

2. Whisk eggs, onion, and one tablespoon of water in a medium bowl.

3. Warm a wok over high warmth.

4. Add a large portion of the sesame oil and a large portion of the nut oil to wok; whirl to cover the surface.

5. Pour into equal parts the egg blend and whirl to shape an omelet.

6. Top with a large portion of the tofu, and other toppings.

7. Sprinkle omelets with dressing.

8. Serve with shallots and coriander.

1.2 Thai Cabbage and Carrot Pancakes Recipe

Preparation time: 25 minutes

Cooking Time: 15 minutes

Serving: 4

Ingredients

- Chopped garlic, two teaspoon
- Green onions, three tablespoon
- Chopped fresh carrots, half cup
- Butter, two tablespoon
- Salt to taste
- Baking soda, one teaspoon
- Black pepper to taste

- Flour, two cups
- Eggs, two
- Chopped onions, two tablespoon
- Milk, one cup
- Chopped fresh cabbage, half cup

Instructions:

1. In a large bowl sift the flour well.
2. Add in the fresh cabbage, green onions, chopped garlic, baking soda, chopped onions, carrots, salt, and pepper.
3. In a separate bowl, mix in the milk and eggs together.
4. Add the milk and egg mixture into the dried mixture.
5. Mix delicately until a smooth texture is formed.
6. In a wok, add the butter and scoop in some amount of the pancake batter.
7. Cook the batter and flip it, making sure both sides are cooked properly.
8. Your dish is ready to be served.

1.3 Thai Cauliflower Pancakes Recipe

Preparation time: 25 minutes

Cooking Time: 15 minutes

Serving: 4

Ingredients

- Chopped garlic, two teaspoon
- Green onions, three tablespoon
- Butter, two tablespoon
- Salt to taste
- Baking soda, one teaspoon
- Black pepper to taste
- Flour, two cups
- Eggs, two
- Chopped onions, two tablespoon
- Milk, one cup
- Chopped fresh cauliflower, half cup

Instructions:

1. In a large bowl, sift the flour well.
2. Add in the fresh chopped cauliflower, green onions, chopped garlic, baking soda, chopped onions, salt, and pepper.
3. In a separate bowl, mix the milk and eggs.
4. Add the milk and egg mixture into the dried mixture.
5. Mix delicately until a smooth texture is formed.
6. In a wok, add the butter and scoop in some amount of the pancake batter.
7. Cook the batter and flip it, making sure both sides are cooked properly.
8. Your dish is ready to be served.

1.4 Thai Buttermilk Biscuits Recipe

Preparation time: 25 minutes

Cooking Time: 20 minutes

Serving: 4-6

Ingredients:

- Honey, two tablespoon
- Unsalted butter, half cup
- All-purpose flour, two cups
- Honey butter topping, two tablespoon
- Salt to taste
- Buttermilk, two cups
- Egg wash, one

Instructions:

1. Make a dough using all the ingredients except the egg wash.
2. Add the butter and the buttermilk at the end of all the ingredients.
3. Knead the dough until it becomes soft and fluffy.
4. Once the dough is done, it is time to make small cake pieces out of the dough.
5. You can cut your dough into round shapes or any other shape you prefer.
6. Place your biscuits on a baking tray.
7. Cover each biscuit with egg wash.

8. Bake your biscuits for fifteen to twenty minutes.

9. Your dish is ready to be served.

1.5 Thai Vegan Congee with Broccoli Recipe

Preparation Time: 10 minutes

Cooking Time: 15 minutes

Serving: 2

Ingredients:

- Rice, one cup
- Sugar, one tablespoon
- Milk, two cups
- Broccoli, one cup
- Cilantro, one tablespoon
- Brown sugar, two teaspoon

Instructions:

1. Mix all ingredients in a wok.
2. Bring to a boil and reduce to medium heat, stirring frequently.
3. Cook for five minutes until the milk is absorbed.
4. Remove from heat and cool for several minutes.
5. Add the cilantro on top.
6. Your dish is ready to be served.

1.6 Thai Quinoa Bowl Recipe

Preparation time: 25 minutes

Cooking Time: 10 minutes

Serving: 4

Ingredients:

- Asian Sesame oil, two tablespoon
- Chopped garlic, two teaspoon
- Green onions, three tablespoon
- Bell pepper strips, half cup
- Quinoa, two cups
- Vegetarian dressing, two tablespoon
- Soy sauce, two tablespoon
- Salt to taste
- Black pepper to taste
- Carrots, two cups
- Boiled eggs, six
- Chopped onions, two tablespoon

Instructions:

1. Cook the quinoa and drain it.
2. Add in all the ingredients in a bowl.
3. Mix the ingredients well and add more dressing if you like.
4. Your dish is ready to be served.

1.7 Thai Breakfast Bake Recipe

Preparation time: 10 minutes

Cooking Time: 20 minutes

Serving: 6

Ingredients:

- Chopped garlic, two teaspoon
- Onions, three tablespoon
- Shredded cheddar cheese, half cup
- Potatoes, two
- Quinoa, one cup
- Vegetable oil, two tablespoon
- Soy sauce, two tablespoon
- Salt to taste
- Black pepper to taste
- Water, half cup
- Eggs, six

Instructions:

1. In a wok, cook the quinoa until properly cooked through.
2. Add garlic, diced potatoes, and water.
3. Add the onion.
4. Add a shower of oil if potatoes begin adhering to the lower part of the dish.

5. Add sausage back to the container.

6. Break eggs into the dish over high warmth and cook it.

7. Add the mixture into a baking dish.

8. Sprinkle cheddar cheese onto the potatoes in a baking dish.

9. Let the cheese melt.

10.   Your dish is fit to be served.

1.8 Thai Vegan Congee with Tofu and Peas Recipe

Preparation Time: 10 minutes

Cooking Time: 15 minutes

Serving: 2

Ingredients:

- Rice, one cup
- Sugar, one tablespoon
- Milk, two cups
- Tofu, one cup
- Cilantro, one tablespoon
- Brown sugar, two teaspoon
- Peas, one cup

Instructions:

1. Mix all ingredients in a pan.
2. Bring to a boil and reduce to medium heat, stirring frequently.
3. Cook for fifteen minutes until the milk is absorbed.
4. Remove from heat and cool it down for several minutes.
5. Add the cilantro on top.
6. Your dish is ready to be served.

1.9 Thai Chili and Eggs Recipe

Preparation time: 20 minutes

Cooking Time: 5 minutes

Serving: 2

Ingredients:

- Asian Sesame oil, two tablespoon
- Tomato, one
- Green onions, three tablespoon
- Soy sauce, half cup
- Chili sauce, one tablespoon
- Chopped fresh coriander, two tablespoon
- Peanut oil, two tablespoon
- Salt to taste
- Black pepper to taste
- Eggs, six

Instructions:

1. Cut the tomato down the middle and cut it into fine pieces.
2. Delicately beat the eggs in a bowl with the sesame oil, a large portion of the spring onion, and salt and pepper to consolidate.
3. Blend the sauces.
4. Warm a wok over high warmth until hot; at that point, add the nut oil.
5. Cook the egg combination until it is firm.

6. Disperse with the excess spring onion and the coriander twigs.

7. At that point, spoon over a portion of the readied sauce.

8. Your dish is fit to be served.

1.10 Thai Vegan Egg Breakfast Sandwich Recipe

Preparation time: 25 minutes

Cooking Time: 15 minutes

Serving: 4

Ingredients:

- Asian Sesame oil, two tablespoon
- Chopped garlic, two teaspoon
- Green onions, three tablespoon
- Tortilla wraps, eight
- Egg, four
- Mixed vegetables, two cups
- Chopped fresh dill, two tablespoon
- Vegetable oil, two tablespoon
- Salt to taste

Instructions:

1. Heat a pan and add in the oil.

2. Add all the cooking ingredients into the pan and cook.

3. Cook your vegetables until they are soft and tender for five to ten minutes.

4. Add in the eggs and cook them.

5. Lay the tortilla wraps with the prepared vegetables and heat them in the pan.

6. Once it is golden brown, remove it.

7. Your dish is ready to be served with your preferred dip.

1.11 Thai Vegan Breakfast Casserole Recipe

Preparation time: 10 minutes

Cooking Time: 20 minutes

Serving: 6

Ingredients:

- Chopped garlic, two teaspoon
- Onions, three tablespoon
- Corn, half cup
- Potatoes, two
- Carrots, one cup
- Bell peppers, one cup
- Vegetable oil, two tablespoon
- Soy sauce, two tablespoon
- Salt to taste
- Black pepper to taste
- Water, half cup
- Eggs, six

Instructions:

1. In a wok, cook the onions until properly cooked through.
2. Add garlic, diced potatoes, and water.
3. Add the rest of the vegetables.
4. Add a shower of oil if potatoes begin adhering to the lower part of the dish.
5. Add the mixture into a baking dish.
6. Break eggs into the dish and mix it.
7. Let the casserole bake for ten to fifteen minutes.
8. Your dish is fit to be served.

1.12 Thai Vegetable Oatmeal Recipe

Preparation Time: 10 minutes

Cooking Time: 15 minutes

Serving: 2

Ingredients:

- Rolled oats, one cup
- Maple syrup, one tablespoon
- Milk, two cups
- Carrot, one cup
- Broccoli, half cup
- Peas, one cup
- Brown sugar, two teaspoon

Instructions:

1. Mix all ingredients except the cilantro in a saucepan.

2. Bring to a boil and reduce to medium heat, stirring frequently.

3. Cook for five minutes until the milk is absorbed.

4. Remove from heat and cool for several minutes.

5. Add the cilantro on top.

6. Your dish is ready to be served.

1.13 Thai Peanut Granola Bars Recipe

Preparation time: 25 minutes

Cooking Time: 15 minutes

Serving: 4

Ingredients:

- Asian Sesame oil, two tablespoon
- Honey, three tablespoon
- Sesame seeds, half cup
- Peanuts, two cups
- Sugar, two tablespoon
- Rice crisp, two cups

Instructions:

1. Mix everything in a bowl except the sugar.

2. Melt the sugar and add it to the above mixture.

3. Lay the mixture in a tray and let it cool down.

4. Cut down the granola bars.

5. Your dish is ready to be served.

1.14 Thai Saffron Rice Recipe

Preparation time: 10 minutes

Cooking Time: 10 minutes

Serving: 4

Ingredients:

- Soy sauce, two tablespoon
- Chopped garlic, two teaspoon
- Green onions, three tablespoon
- Mixed vegetables, half cup
- Saffron, one teaspoon
- Asian sesame oil, one tablespoon
- Vegetable oil, two tablespoon
- Salt to taste
- Black pepper to taste
- Cooked rice, two cups

Instructions:

1. Warm a pan.
2. Add about a tablespoon of oil.
3. Add the onions.
4. Add in the garlic when onions are done.
5. Add the diced or cut vegetables and mix until daintily cooked.

6. Add your rice, somewhat more oil if you need it, and mix.

7. Add about a teaspoon of saffron to the pan.

8. Add in the Asian sesame oil.

9. Mix everything.

10. Sprinkle green onions on top.

11. Your dish is ready to be served.

1.15 Spicy Thai Vegan Scramble Recipe

Preparation time: 25 minutes

Cooking Time: 15 minutes

Serving: 4

Ingredients:

- Chopped garlic, two teaspoon
- Green onions, three tablespoon
- Tomato, half cup
- Cauliflower, two cups
- Chopped fresh dill, two tablespoon
- Vegetable oil, two tablespoon
- Soy sauce, two tablespoon
- Salt to taste
- Black pepper to taste
- Carrots, two cups
- Eggs, eight
- Chopped onions, two tablespoon

Instructions:

1. Warm the oil in a wok and cook the garlic and onions.

2. Add the carrots and cook them on medium-high warmth for several seconds or until they begin to take on a changed tone.

3. Add in the cauliflower and tomato cook until delicate, however to some degree crispy.

4. Turn down the warmth and pour the beaten eggs and leave to set for a couple of moments.

5. At the point when the entirety of the egg has set, tip in the soy sauce and chopped dill, and let it sizzle for a couple of moments.

6. Season with some salt and pepper.

7. Your dish is ready to be served.

1.16 Thai Braised Plantain Recipe

Preparation time: 10 minutes

Cooking Time: 5 minutes

Serving: 4

Ingredients:

- Asian Sesame oil, two tablespoon
- Chopped garlic, two teaspoon
- Thai spice, two tablespoon
- Soy sauce, two tablespoon
- Salt to taste
- Black pepper to taste
- Plantain cubes, two cups

Instructions:

1. Heat a wok on medium flame.
2. Add the oil and garlic.
3. Cook the garlic, once browned, add the plantain, and mix Thai spice into it.
4. After the plantain is half cooked, add the soy sauce, salt, and pepper.
5. Cook more for ten minutes.
6. Your dish is ready to be served.

1.17 Thai Pomelo Salad Recipe

Preparation time: 25 minutes

Cooking Time: 5 minutes

Serving: 4

Ingredients:

- Asian Sesame oil, two tablespoon
- Chopped garlic, two teaspoon
- Green onions, three tablespoon
- Coconut flakes, half cup
- Cabbage, two cups
- Chili dressing, two tablespoon
- Soy sauce, two tablespoon
- Salt to taste
- Black pepper to taste
- Peanuts, two cups
- Lime juice, two tablespoon

Instructions:

1. Cut all the things in the same way.
2. Add in all the ingredients in a bowl.
3. Mix the ingredients well and add more dressing if you like.
4. Your dish is ready to be served.

Chapter 2: Veggie Thai Lunch Recipes

In this chapter you will learn some amazing Thai vegetarian lunch dishes that you can easy make at home on your own.

2.1 Thai Basil Eggplant Recipe

Preparation time: 25 minutes

Cooking Time: 15 minutes

Serving: 4

Ingredients:

- Hoisin sauce, two tablespoon
- Chopped garlic, two teaspoon
- Corn starch, three tablespoon
- Vegetable broth, half cup
- Eggplant, two cups
- Brown sugar, two tablespoon
- Fresh basil leaves, one cup
- Vegetable oil, two tablespoon
- Soy sauce, two tablespoon
- Salt to taste
- Black pepper to taste
- Chopped onions, two tablespoon

Instructions:

1. In a small bowl, combine the cloves, brown sugar, corn starch, soy sauce, hoisin sauce, ginger, and vegetable broth until blended.

2. Heat a large pan.

3. Stir-fry the eggplant in remaining oil until they are crisp-tender.

4. Stir cornstarch mixture.

5. Bring to a boil; cook until thickened, and add the basil leaves.

6. Let it cook for a few minutes until all the moisture from the dish steams out.

7. Your dish is ready to be served.

2.2 Thai Red Curry Lentils Recipes

Preparation time: 10 minutes

Cooking Time: 10 minutes

Serving: 4

Ingredients:

- Soy sauce, two tablespoon
- Chopped garlic, two teaspoon
- Green onions, three tablespoon
- Red lentils, two cups
- Red curry paste, one tablespoon
- Chopped onions, one cup
- Asian sesame oil, one tablespoon
- Vegetable oil, two tablespoon
- Salt to taste

- Black pepper to taste
- Vegetable broth, two cups
- Cilantro, one tablespoon

Instructions:

1. Warm a wok.
2. Add about a tablespoon of oil.
3. Add the onions
4. Fry them, and then add garlic.
5. Add the red lentils and mix.
6. Add the red curry paste.
7. Add somewhat more oil if you need it and mix.
8. Add about a teaspoon of soy sauce to the wok.
9. Add in the salt and pepper.
10. Add the vegetable broth into the wok.
11. Let it cook until a thick curry forms.
12. Garnish with cilantro and green onions.
13. Plate and serve quickly.

2.3 Thai Coconut Cauliflower Soup Recipe

Preparation time: 10 minutes

Cooking Time: 10 minutes

Serving: 4

Ingredients:

- Soy sauce, two tablespoon

- Chopped garlic, two teaspoon
- Green onions, three tablespoon
- Cauliflower florets, half cup
- Coconut milk, one cup
- Asian sesame oil, one tablespoon
- Vegetable oil, two tablespoon
- Salt to taste
- Black pepper to taste
- Vegetable stock, two cups
- Cilantro, one tablespoon

Instructions:

1. Warm a wok.
2. Add about a tablespoon of oil.
3. Add the diced or cut cauliflower florets and mix until daintily cooked.
4. Add the ginger and garlic to the vegetables.
5. Add your coconut milk, somewhat more of it if you need it, and mix.
6. Add about a teaspoon of soy sauce to the wok.
7. Add in the vegetable stock and Asian sesame oil into the wok.
8. Add in the rest of the ingredients.
9. Mix everything.
10. Top it with cilantro leaves.
11. Plate and serve quickly with more soy sauce.

2.4 Thai Almond Coconut Rice with Ginger Peanut Sauce Recipe

Preparation time: 10 minutes

Cooking Time: 10 minutes

Serving: 4

Ingredients:

- Soy sauce, two tablespoon
- Chopped garlic, two teaspoon
- Green onions, three tablespoon
- Almonds, half cup
- Coconut essence, one tablespoon
- Ginger peanut sauce, one cup
- Asian sesame oil, one tablespoon
- Vegetable oil, two tablespoon
- Salt to taste
- Black pepper to taste
- Cooked rice, two cups

Instructions:

1. Warm a pan.
2. Add about a tablespoon of oil.
3. Add the almonds.
4. Fry them and remove them to a plate.

5. Add the cooked rice and mix.

6. Add the ginger peanut sauce.

7. Add your rice, somewhat more oil if you need it, and mix.

8. Add about a teaspoon of soy sauce to the pan.

9. Mix the ginger peanut sauce into the pan.

10. Add the coconut essence and almonds into the pan.

11. Garnish it with green onions.

12. Plate and serve quickly.

2.5 Thai Coconut and Tofu Soup Recipe

Preparation time: 10 minutes

Cooking Time: 10 minutes

Serving: 4

Ingredients:

- Soy sauce, two tablespoon
- Chopped garlic, two teaspoon
- Green onions, three tablespoon
- Tofu cubes, half cup
- Coconut milk, one cup
- Asian sesame oil, one tablespoon
- Vegetable oil, two tablespoon
- Salt to taste
- Black pepper to taste
- Vegetable stock, two cups
- Cilantro, one tablespoon

Instructions:

1. Warm a wok.
2. Add about a tablespoon of oil.
3. Add the diced or cut tofu cubes and mix until daintily cooked.
4. Add the ginger and garlic to the vegetables.
5. Add your coconut milk, somewhat more of it if you need it, and mix.
6. Add about a teaspoon of soy sauce to the wok.
7. Add in the vegetable stock and Asian sesame oil into the wok.
8. Add in the rest of the ingredients.
9. Mix everything.
10. Top it with cilantro leaves.
11. Your dish is ready to be served.

2.6 Zucchini Noodle Pad Thai Recipe

Preparation time: 25 minutes

Cooking Time: 15 minutes

Serving: 4

Ingredients:

- Asian Sesame oil, two tablespoon
- Chopped garlic, two teaspoon
- Green onions, three tablespoon
- Tomatoes, half cup
- Chopped fresh dill, two tablespoon
- Vegetable oil, two tablespoon
- Soy sauce, two tablespoon
- Salt to taste
- Black pepper to taste
- Zucchini, two cups
- Corn flour, two tablespoon
- Mix Thai spices, one tablespoon
- Chopped onions, two tablespoon
- Spaghetti noodles, one pack.

Instructions:

1. Heat a wok on medium flame.
2. Add in the oil and let it heat up.
3. Add the onions and cook it until translucent.
4. Add in the garlic and cook it for two minutes.
5. Add in the tomatoes and cook it for five minutes.
6. Add in the zucchini.
7. Add the soy sauce, mix Thai spices, salt and pepper into the wok and cook for five minutes.
8. Let the mixture cook for about ten minutes until a thick mixture is formed.

9. Add in the noodles.

10. Cover the mixture for five minutes.

11. Add in the sesame oil, green onions, and fresh chopped dill on top.

12. Your dish is ready to be served.

2.7 Thai Noodles with Crunchy Kale Recipe

Preparation time: 25 minutes

Cooking Time: 15 minutes

Serving: 4

Ingredients:

- Asian Sesame oil, two tablespoon
- Chopped garlic, two teaspoon
- Green onions, three tablespoon
- Tomatoes, half cup
- Chopped fresh dill, two tablespoon
- Vegetable oil, two tablespoon
- Soy sauce, two tablespoon
- Salt to taste
- Black pepper to taste
- Kale, two cups
- Corn flour, two tablespoon
- Mix Thai spices, one tablespoon
- Chopped onions, two tablespoon
- Spaghetti noodles, one pack.

Instructions:

1. Heat a wok on medium flame.

2. Add in the oil and let it heat up.

3. Add the onions and cook it until translucent.

4. Add in the garlic and cook it for two minutes.

5. Add in the tomatoes and cook it for five minutes.

6. Add in the kale.

7. Add the soy sauce, mix Thai spices, salt and pepper into the wok and cook for five minutes.

8. Let the mixture cook for about ten minutes until a thick mixture is formed.

9. Add in the noodles.

10. Cover the mixture for five minutes.

11. Add in the sesame oil, green onions, and fresh chopped dill on top.

12. Your dish is ready to be served.

2.8 Thai Vegan Peanut Curry Recipe

Preparation time: 10 minutes

Cooking Time: 10 minutes

Serving: 4

Ingredients:

- Soy sauce, two tablespoon
- Chopped garlic, two teaspoon
- Green onions, three tablespoon
- Peanuts, two cups

- Chopped onions, one cup
- Asian sesame oil, one tablespoon
- Vegetable oil, two tablespoon
- Salt to taste
- Black pepper to taste
- Vegetable broth, two cups
- Cilantro, one tablespoon

Instructions:

1. Warm a wok.
2. Add about a tablespoon of oil.
3. Add the onions
4. Fry them, and then add garlic.
5. Add the peanuts and mix.
6. Add somewhat more oil if you need it and mix.
7. Add about a teaspoon of soy sauce to the wok.
8. Add in the salt and pepper.
9. Add the vegetable broth into the wok.
10. Let it cook until a thick curry forms.
11. Garnish with cilantro and green onions.
12. Plate and serve quickly.

2.9 Thai Peanut Ramen Noodle Soup Recipe

Preparation time: 10 minutes

Cooking Time: 10 minutes

Serving: 4

Ingredients:

- Soy sauce, two tablespoon
- Chopped garlic, two teaspoon
- Green onions, three tablespoon
- Peanuts, two cups
- Ramen, four packs
- Chopped onions, one cup
- Asian sesame oil, one tablespoon
- Vegetable oil, two tablespoon
- Salt to taste
- Black pepper to taste
- Vegetable broth, three cups
- Cilantro, one tablespoon

Instructions:

1. Warm a wok.
2. Add about a tablespoon of oil.
3. Add the onions
4. Fry them, and then add garlic.
5. Add the peanuts and mix.
6. Add the ramen.
7. Add somewhat more oil if you need it and mix.
8. Add about a teaspoon of soy sauce to the wok.
9. Add in the salt and pepper.
10. Add the vegetable broth into the wok.

11.   Let it cook until a thick curry forms.

12.   Garnish with cilantro and green onions.

13.   Plate and serve quickly.

2.10 Thai Tofu Green Curry Skewers with Peanut Sauce Recipe

Preparation time: 25 minutes

Cooking Time: 10 minutes

Serving Size: 4

Ingredients:

- Eggplant, one
- Pineapple, one can
- Tofu, two ounces
- Wooden skewers
- Maple syrup, one tablespoon
- Peanut butter, half cup
- Thai green curry paste, two tablespoon
- Rice vinegar, one teaspoon
- Soy sauce, two tablespoon
- Garlic and ginger paste, one teaspoon

Instructions:

1. Blend all of the marinade ingredients.
2. Cut the squash, pineapple, and eggplant, and divide the pieces into eight equal piles.
3. Cut the tofu and add the pieces to the piles.

4. Place the squash, pineapple, and eggplant, and tofu on the skewers, alternating as you go.

5. Lay these skewers on a baking sheet, and brush with some of the marinade.

6. Grill on medium-high, or broil on high on a baking sheet or broiler pan.

7. Brush the marinade again if the skewers dry out.

8. Your kebabs are ready to be served.

2.11 Vegan Thai Basil Noodles Recipe

Preparation time: 25 minutes

Cooking Time: 15 minutes

Serving: 4

Ingredients:

- Asian Sesame oil, two tablespoon
- Chopped garlic, two teaspoon
- Green onions, three tablespoon
- Tomatoes, half cup
- Chopped fresh dill, two tablespoon
- Vegetable oil, two tablespoon
- Soy sauce, two tablespoon

- Salt to taste
- Black pepper to taste
- Basil leaves, two cups
- Corn flour, two tablespoon
- Mix Thai spices, one tablespoon
- Chopped onions, two tablespoon
- Spaghetti noodles, one pack

Instructions:

1. Heat a wok on medium flame.
2. Add in the oil and let it heat up.
3. Add the onions and cook it until translucent.
4. Add in the garlic and cook it for two minutes.
5. Add in the tomatoes and cook it for five minutes.
6. Add in the basil leaves.
7. Add the soy sauce, mix Thai spices, salt and pepper into the wok and cook for five minutes.
8. Let the mixture cook for about ten minutes until a thick mixture is formed.
9. Add in the noodles.
10. Cover the mixture for five minutes.
11. Add in the sesame oil, green onions, and fresh chopped dill on top.
12. Your dish is ready to be served.

2.12 Thai Green Avocado Curry Recipe

Preparation time: 10 minutes

Cooking Time: 10 minutes

Serving: 4

Ingredients:

- Soy sauce, two tablespoon
- Chopped garlic, two teaspoon
- Green onions, three tablespoon
- Red lentils, two cups
- Red curry paste, one tablespoon
- Chopped onions, one cup
- Asian sesame oil, one tablespoon
- Vegetable oil, two tablespoon
- Salt to taste
- Black pepper to taste
- Vegetable broth, two cups
- Cilantro, one tablespoon

Instructions:

1. Warm a wok.
2. Add about a tablespoon of oil.
3. Add the onions
4. Add the green curry paste and mix.
5. Add the avocado cubes.

6. Add about a teaspoon of soy sauce to the wok.

7. Add in the salt and pepper.

8. Add the vegetable broth into the wok.

9. Let it cook until a thick curry forms.

10. Garnish with cilantro and green onions.

11. Plate and serve quickly.

2.13 Thai Spicy Peanut Ramen Recipe

Preparation time: 10 minutes

Cooking Time: 10 minutes

Serving: 4

Ingredients:

- Soy sauce, two tablespoon
- Chopped garlic, two teaspoon
- Green onions, three tablespoon
- Peanuts, two cups
- Ramen, four packs
- Red chili paste, two tablespoon
- Chopped onions, one cup
- Asian sesame oil, one tablespoon
- Vegetable oil, two tablespoon
- Salt to taste
- Black pepper to taste
- Cilantro, one tablespoon

Instructions:

1. Warm a wok.
2. Add about a tablespoon of oil.
3. Add the onions
4. Add garlic and red chili paste.
5. Add the peanuts and mix.
6. Add the ramen.
7. Add about a teaspoon of soy sauce to the wok.
8. Add in the salt and pepper.
9. Garnish with cilantro and green onions.
10. Plate and serve quickly.

2.14 Thai Red Curry with Cauliflower and Potatoes Recipe

Preparation time: 10 minutes

Cooking Time: 10 minutes

Serving: 4

Ingredients:

- Soy sauce, two tablespoon
- Chopped garlic, two teaspoon
- Green onions, three tablespoon
- Cauliflower and potatoes, two cups (one cup each)
- Red curry paste, one tablespoon
- Chopped onions, one cup
- Asian sesame oil, one tablespoon
- Vegetable oil, two tablespoon
- Salt to taste

- Black pepper to taste
- Vegetable broth, two cups
- Cilantro, one tablespoon

Instructions:

1. Warm a wok.
2. Add about a tablespoon of oil.
3. Add the onions
4. Add the cauliflower, potatoes, and mix.
5. Add the red curry paste.
6. Add about a teaspoon of soy sauce to the wok.
7. Add in the salt and pepper.
8. Add the vegetable broth into the wok.
9. Let it cook until a thick curry forms.
10. Garnish with cilantro and green onions.
11. Plate and serve quickly.

2.15 Spicy Thai Chickpea and Broccoli Salad Recipe

Preparation time: 25 minutes

Cooking Time: 5 minutes

Serving: 4

Ingredients:

- Asian Sesame oil, two tablespoon
- Chopped garlic, two teaspoon
- Green onions, three tablespoon
- Broccoli, two cups
- Thai spicy dressing, two tablespoon
- Soy sauce, two tablespoon
- Salt to taste
- Black pepper to taste
- Chickpeas, two cups
- Lime juice, two tablespoon

Instructions:

1. Cut all the things in the same way.
2. Add in all the ingredients in a bowl.
3. Mix the ingredients well and add more dressing if you like.
4. Your dish is ready to be served.

2.16 Thai Vegan Ramen Recipe

Preparation time: 10 minutes

Cooking Time: 10 minutes

Serving: 4

Ingredients:

- Soy sauce, two tablespoon
- Chopped garlic, two teaspoon
- Green onions, three tablespoon
- Mixed vegetables, two cups
- Ramen, four packs
- Red chili paste, two tablespoon
- Chopped onions, one cup
- Asian sesame oil, one tablespoon
- Vegetable oil, two tablespoon
- Salt to taste
- Black pepper to taste
- Cilantro, one tablespoon

Instructions:

1. Warm a wok.
2. Add about a tablespoon of oil.
3. Add the onions
4. Add garlic and red chili paste.
5. Add the vegetables and mix.
6. Add the ramen.

7. Add about a teaspoon of soy sauce to the wok.

8. Add in the salt and pepper.

9. Garnish with cilantro and green onions.

10. Plate and serve quickly.

2.17 Thai Vegan Green Curry Soup Recipe

Preparation time: 10 minutes

Cooking Time: 10 minutes

Serving: 4

Ingredients:

- Soy sauce, two tablespoon
- Chopped garlic, two teaspoon
- Green curry paste, three tablespoon
- Mix vegetables, two cups
- Chopped onions, one cup
- Asian sesame oil, one tablespoon
- Vegetable oil, two tablespoon
- Salt to taste
- Black pepper to taste
- Vegetable broth, three cups
- Cilantro, one tablespoon

Instructions:

1. Warm a wok.
2. Add about a tablespoon of oil.
3. Add the onions

4. Fry them, and then add garlic.

5. Add the vegetables and mix.

6. Add the green curry paste.

7. Add about a teaspoon of soy sauce to the wok.

8. Add in the salt and pepper.

9. Add the vegetable broth into the wok.

10. Let it cook until a thick soup forms.

11. Garnish with cilantro.

12. Plate and serve quickly.

2.18 Chopped Thai Broccoli Salad Recipe

Preparation time: 25 minutes

Cooking Time: 5 minutes

Serving: 4

Ingredients:

- Asian Sesame oil, two tablespoon
- Chopped garlic, two teaspoon
- Green onions, three tablespoon
- Broccoli, two cups
- Thai spicy dressing, two tablespoon
- Soy sauce, two tablespoon
- Salt to taste
- Black pepper to taste
- Lime juice, two tablespoon

Instructions:

1. Cut all the things in the same way.
2. Add in all the ingredients in a bowl.
3. Mix the ingredients well and add more dressing if you like.
4. Your dish is ready to be served.

2.19 Vegan Thai Peanut Pasta Salad Recipe

Preparation time: 25 minutes

Cooking Time: 5 minutes

Serving: 4

Ingredients:

- Asian Sesame oil, two tablespoon
- Chopped garlic, two teaspoon
- Green onions, three tablespoon
- Pasta, two cups
- Thai spicy dressing, two tablespoon
- Soy sauce, two tablespoon
- Salt to taste
- Black pepper to taste
- Peanuts, two cups
- Lime juice, two tablespoon

Instructions:

1. Cut all the things in the same way.
2. Add in all the ingredients in a bowl.

3. Mix the ingredients well and add more dressing if you like.

4. Your dish is ready to be served.

2.20 Thai Carrot and Ginger Soup with Cashews Recipe

Preparation time: 10 minutes

Cooking Time: 10 minutes

Serving: 4

Ingredients:

- Soy sauce, two tablespoon
- Chopped ginger, two teaspoon
- Carrots, two cups
- Fried cashews, one cup
- Asian sesame oil, one tablespoon
- Vegetable oil, two tablespoon
- Salt to taste
- Black pepper to taste
- Vegetable broth, three cups
- Cilantro, one tablespoon

Instructions:

1. Warm a wok.
2. Add about a tablespoon of oil.
3. Fry them, and then add ginger.
4. Add the carrots and mix.
5. Add the fried cashews.
6. Add about a teaspoon of soy sauce to the wok.

7. Add in the salt and pepper.

8. Add the vegetable broth into the wok.

9. Let it cook until a thick soup forms.

10.   Garnish with cilantro.

11.   Plate and serve quickly.

Chapter 3: Veggie Thai Dinner Recipes

In this chapter you will learn some amazing Thai vegetarian dinner dishes that you can easy make at home on your own.

3.1 Thai Crispy Tofu Noodles Recipe

Preparation time: 25 minutes

Cooking Time: 15 minutes

Serving: 4

Ingredients:

- Asian Sesame oil, two tablespoon
- Chopped garlic, two teaspoon
- Green onions, three tablespoon
- Tomatoes, half cup
- Chopped fresh dill, two tablespoon
- Vegetable oil, two tablespoon
- Soy sauce, two tablespoon
- Salt to taste
- Black pepper to taste
- Fried tofu, two cups
- Corn flour, two tablespoon
- Mix Thai spices, one tablespoon
- Chopped onions, two tablespoon
- Spaghetti noodles, one pack.

Instructions:

1. Heat a wok on medium flame.
2. Add in the oil and let it heat up.
3. Add the onions and cook it until translucent.
4. Add in the garlic and cook it for two minutes.
5. Add in the tomatoes and cook it for five minutes.
6. Add in the fried Tofu.
7. Add the soy sauce, mix Thai spices, salt and pepper into the wok and cook for five minutes.
8. Let the mixture cook for about ten minutes until a thick mixture is formed.
9. Add in the noodles.
10. Cover the mixture for five minutes.
11. Add in the sesame oil, green onions, and fresh chopped dill on top.
12. Your dish is ready to be served.

3.2 Thai Black pepper and Garlic Tofu Recipe

Preparation time: 10 minutes

Cooking Time: 5 minutes

Serving: 4

Ingredients:

- Asian Sesame oil, two tablespoon
- Chopped garlic, four teaspoon
- Thai spice, two tablespoon
- Soy sauce, two tablespoon
- Salt to taste

- Tofu cubes, two cups
- Corn flour, two tablespoon
- Vegetable stock, half cup
- Crushed black pepper, one tablespoon
- Cilantro, one tablespoon

Instructions:

1. Heat a wok on medium flame.
2. Add the oil and garlic.
3. Cook the garlic, once browned, add the tofu, and mix Thai spice into it.
4. After the tofu is half cooked, add the soy sauce and salt.
5. Add in the crushed black pepper, cornflour, and vegetable stock.
6. Cook for a further ten minutes.
7. Add the cilantro on top.
8. Your dish is ready to be served.

3.3 Thai Basil Fried Rice Recipe

Preparation time: 25 minutes

Cooking Time: 15 minutes

Serving: 4

Ingredients:

- Asian Sesame oil, two tablespoon
- Chopped garlic, two teaspoon
- Green onions, three tablespoon

- Tomatoes, half cup
- Chopped fresh dill, two tablespoon
- Vegetable oil, two tablespoon
- Soy sauce, two tablespoon
- Salt to taste
- Black pepper to taste
- Basil leaves, two cups
- Corn flour, two tablespoon
- Mix Thai spices, one tablespoon
- Chopped onions, two tablespoon
- Cooked rice, two cups

Instructions:

1. Heat a wok on medium flame.
2. Add in the oil and let it heat up.
3. Add the onions and cook it until translucent.
4. Add in the garlic and cook it for two minutes.
5. Add in the tomatoes and cook it for five minutes.
6. Add in the basil leaves.
7. Add the soy sauce, mix Thai spices, salt and pepper into the wok and cook for five minutes.
8. Let the mixture cook for about ten minutes until a thick mixture is formed.
9. Add in the cooked rice.
10. Cover the mixture for five minutes.

11.   Add in the sesame oil, green onions, and fresh chopped dill on top.

12.   Your dish is ready to be served.

3.4 Thai Raw Vegan Pad Thai Recipe

Preparation time: 25 minutes

Cooking Time: 5 minutes

Serving: 4

Ingredients:

- Asian Sesame oil, two tablespoon
- Chopped garlic, two teaspoon
- Green onions, three tablespoon
- Glass noodles, two cups
- Thai spicy dressing, two tablespoon
- Soy sauce, two tablespoon
- Salt to taste
- Black pepper to taste
- Raw mixed vegetables, two cups
- Lime juice, two tablespoon

Instructions:

1. Cut all the things in the same way.
2. Add in all the ingredients in a bowl.

3. Mix the ingredients well and add more sauces if you like.

4. Your dish is ready to be served.

3.5 Thai Coconut Lime Soup Recipe

Preparation time: 10 minutes

Cooking Time: 10 minutes

Serving: 4

Ingredients:

- Soy sauce, two tablespoon
- Chopped garlic, two teaspoon
- Green onions, three tablespoon
- Lime juice, half cup
- Coconut milk, one cup
- Asian sesame oil, one tablespoon
- Vegetable oil, two tablespoon
- Salt to taste
- Black pepper to taste
- Vegetable stock, two cups
- Cilantro, one tablespoon
- Shredded coconut flakes, half cup

Instructions:

1. Warm a wok.
2. Add about a tablespoon of oil.
3. Add the ginger and garlic to the vegetables.

4. Add your coconut milk, somewhat more of it if you need it, and mix.

5. Add in the lime juice and shredded coconut.

6. Add about a teaspoon of soy sauce to the wok.

7. Add in the vegetable stock and Asian sesame oil into the wok.

8. Add in the rest of the ingredients.

9. Mix everything.

10.   Top it with cilantro leaves.

11.   Your dish is ready to be served.

3.6 Thai Pineapple Fried Rice Recipe

Preparation time: 25 minutes

Cooking Time: 15 minutes

Serving: 4

Ingredients:

- Asian Sesame oil, two tablespoon
- Chopped garlic, two teaspoon
- Green onions, three tablespoon
- Tomatoes, half cup
- Chopped fresh dill, two tablespoon
- Vegetable oil, two tablespoon
- Soy sauce, two tablespoon
- Salt to taste
- Black pepper to taste
- Pineapple chunks, two cups

- Corn flour, two tablespoon
- Mix Thai spices, one tablespoon
- Chopped onions, two tablespoon
- Cooked rice, two cups

Instructions:

1. Heat a wok on medium flame.
2. Add in the oil and let it heat up.
3. Add the onions and cook it until translucent.
4. Add in the garlic and cook it for two minutes.
5. Add in the tomatoes and cook it for five minutes.
6. Add in the pineapple chunks.
7. Add the soy sauce, mix Thai spices, salt and pepper into the wok and cook for five minutes.
8. Let the mixture cook for about ten minutes until a thick mixture is formed.
9. Add in the cooked rice.
10. Cover the mixture for five minutes.
11. Add in the sesame oil, green onions, and fresh chopped dill on top.
12. Your dish is ready to be served.

3.7 Thai Spicy Butternut Squash Soup Recipe

Preparation time: 10 minutes

Cooking Time: 10 minutes

Serving: 4

Ingredients:

- Chopped garlic, two teaspoon
- Green onions, three tablespoon
- Butternut squash, one
- Coconut milk, one cup
- Red chili paste, one tablespoon
- Vegetable oil, two tablespoon
- Salt to taste
- Black pepper to taste
- Vegetable stock, two cups
- Cilantro, one tablespoon

Instructions:

1. Warm a wok.
2. Add about a tablespoon of oil.
3. Add the ginger and garlic to the vegetables.
4. Add your coconut milk, somewhat more of it if you need it, and mix.
5. Add in the butternut squash chunks and red chili paste.
6. Add in the vegetable stock and Asian sesame oil into the wok.
7. Mix everything.
8. Top it with cilantro leaves.
9. Your dish is ready to be served.

3.8 Thai Vegan Rice Salad Recipe

Preparation time: 25 minutes

Cooking Time: 5 minutes

Serving: 4

Ingredients:

- Asian Sesame oil, two tablespoon
- Chopped garlic, two teaspoon
- Green onions, three tablespoon
- Thai salad dressing, two tablespoon
- Soy sauce, two tablespoon
- Salt to taste
- Black pepper to taste
- Rice puffs, two cups
- Lime juice, two tablespoon

Instructions:

1. Cut all the things in the same way.
2. Add in all the ingredients in a bowl.
3. Mix the ingredients well and add more dressing if you like.
4. Your dish is ready to be served.

3.9 Thai Creamy Red Sweet Potato Curry Recipe

Preparation time: 10 minutes

Cooking Time: 10 minutes

Serving: 4

Ingredients:

- Soy sauce, two tablespoon
- Chopped garlic, two teaspoon
- Green onions, three tablespoon
- Sweet potatoes, two cups
- Red curry paste, one tablespoon
- Chopped onions, one cup
- Asian sesame oil, one tablespoon
- Vegetable oil, two tablespoon
- Salt to taste
- Black pepper to taste
- Vegetable broth, two cups
- Cilantro, one tablespoon

Instructions:

1. Warm a wok.
2. Add about a tablespoon of oil.
3. Add the onions
4. Add the sweet potatoes, cream, and mix.
5. Add the red curry paste.

6. Add about a teaspoon of soy sauce to the wok.

7. Add in the salt and pepper.

8. Add the vegetable broth into the wok.

9. Let it cook until a thick curry forms.

10. Garnish with cilantro and green onions.

11. Plate and serve quickly.

3.10 Thai Brussel Sprouts Salad Recipe

Preparation time: 25 minutes

Cooking Time: 5 minutes

Serving: 4

Ingredients:

- Asian Sesame oil, two tablespoon
- Chopped garlic, two teaspoon
- Green onions, three tablespoon
- Thai salad dressing, two tablespoon
- Soy sauce, two tablespoon
- Salt to taste
- Black pepper to taste
- Brussel sprouts, two cups
- Lime juice, two tablespoon

Instructions:

1. Cut all the things in the same way.

2. Add in all the ingredients in a bowl.

3. Mix the ingredients well and add more dressing if you like.

4. Your dish is ready to be served.

3.11 Thai Vegan Green Curry Risotto Recipe

Preparation time: 10 minutes

Cooking Time: 5 minutes

Serving: 4

Ingredients:

- Asian Sesame oil, two tablespoon
- Chopped garlic, four teaspoon
- Thai spice, two tablespoon
- Soy sauce, two tablespoon
- Salt to taste
- Mixed vegetables, two cups
- Fish sauce, two tablespoon
- Coconut cream, half cup
- Shallots, half cup
- Corn flour, two tablespoon
- Vegetable stock, half cup
- Crushed black pepper, one tablespoon
- Cilantro, one tablespoon

Instructions:

1. Heat a wok on medium flame.
2. Add the oil and garlic.

3. Cook the garlic, once browned, add the mixed vegetables, and mix Thai spice into it.

4. After the mixed vegetables are half cooked, add the soy sauce and salt.

5. Add in the crushed black pepper, cornflour, and vegetable stock.

6. Add in the coconut cream and fish sauce.

7. Cook for a further ten minutes.

8. Add the cilantro and shallots on top.

9. Your dish is ready to be served.

3.12 Thai Tofu and Eggplant Stir Fry Recipe

Preparation time: 10 minutes

Cooking Time: 5 minutes

Serving: 4

Ingredients:

- Asian Sesame oil, two tablespoon
- Chopped garlic, four teaspoon
- Thai spice, two tablespoon
- Soy sauce, two tablespoon
- Salt to taste
- Tofu cubes, two cups
- Eggplant, two cups
- Corn flour, two tablespoon
- Vegetable stock, half cup
- Crushed black pepper, one tablespoon

- Cilantro, one tablespoon

Instructions:

1. Heat a wok on medium flame.
2. Add the oil and garlic.
3. Cook the garlic, once browned, add the tofu, and mix Thai spice into it.
4. After the tofu is half cooked, add the soy sauce and salt.
5. Add in the eggplant, crushed black pepper, cornflour, and vegetable stock.
6. Cook for a further ten minutes.
7. Add the cilantro on top.
8. Your dish is ready to be served.

3.13 Thai Vegan Buddha Bowl Recipe

Preparation time: 25 minutes

Cooking Time: 5 minutes

Serving: 4

Ingredients:

- Asian Sesame oil, two tablespoon
- Chopped garlic, two teaspoon
- Green onions, three tablespoon
- Edamame, two cups

- Brown rice, two cups
- Cooked peas, one cup
- Broccoli, one cup
- Red cabbage, one cup
- Avocados, two
- Thai creamy dressing, two tablespoon
- Soy sauce, two tablespoon
- Salt to taste
- Black pepper to taste
- Peanuts, two cups
- Lime juice, two tablespoon

Instructions:

5. Cut all the things in the same way.
6. Add in all the ingredients in a bowl.
7. Mix the ingredients well and add more dressing if you like.
8. Your dish is ready to be served.

3.14 Thai Green Sweet Potato Curry Recipe

Preparation time: 10 minutes

Cooking Time: 10 minutes

Serving: 4

Ingredients:

- Soy sauce, two tablespoon
- Chopped garlic, two teaspoon
- Green onions, three tablespoon
- Sweet potatoes, two cups
- Green curry paste, one tablespoon
- Chopped onions, one cup
- Asian sesame oil, one tablespoon
- Vegetable oil, two tablespoon
- Salt to taste
- Black pepper to taste
- Vegetable broth, two cups
- Cilantro, one tablespoon

Instructions:

1. Warm a wok.
2. Add about a tablespoon of oil.
3. Add the onions
4. Add the sweet potatoes, cream, and mix.
5. Add the green curry paste.
6. Add about a teaspoon of soy sauce to the wok.
7. Add in the salt and pepper.

8. Add the vegetable broth into the wok.

9. Let it cook until a thick curry forms.

10.   Garnish with cilantro and green onions.

11.   Plate and serve quickly.

3.15 Thai Vegetarian Noodles Green Curry Pea Soup Recipe

Preparation time: 10 minutes

Cooking Time: 10 minutes

Serving: 4

Ingredients:

- Soy sauce, two tablespoon
- Chopped garlic, two teaspoon
- Green onions, three tablespoon
- Green peas, two cups
- Noodles, one pack
- Chopped onions, one cup
- Asian sesame oil, one tablespoon
- Vegetable oil, two tablespoon
- Salt to taste
- Black pepper to taste
- Vegetable broth, three cups
- Green curry paste, two tablespoon
- Cilantro, one tablespoon

Instructions:

1. Warm a wok.
2. Add about a tablespoon of oil.
3. Add the onions
4. Fry them, and then add garlic.
5. Add the green peas and mix.
6. Add the green curry paste.
7. Add the noodles.
8. Add somewhat more oil if you need it and mix.
9. Add about a teaspoon of soy sauce to the wok.
10. Add in the salt and pepper.
11. Add the vegetable broth into the wok.
12. Let it cook until a thick soup forms.
13. Garnish with cilantro and green onions.
14. Plate and serve quickly.

3.16 Thai Coconut Apple Kale Salad Recipe

Preparation time: 25 minutes

Cooking Time: 5 minutes

Serving: 4

Ingredients:

- Asian Sesame oil, two tablespoon
- Chopped garlic, two teaspoon
- Green onions, three tablespoon
- Apple, two cups
- Kale, two cups
- Corn, one cup

- Green cabbage, one cup
- Red cabbage, one cup
- Avocados, two
- Thai creamy dressing, two tablespoon
- Soy sauce, two tablespoon
- Salt to taste
- Black pepper to taste
- Coconut milk, two cups
- Lime juice, two tablespoon
- Coconut flakes, half cup

Instructions:

1. Cut all the things in the same way.
2. Add in all the ingredients in a bowl.
3. Mix the ingredients well and add more dressing if you like.
4. Your dish is ready to be served.

3.17 Thai Vegan Tempeh Soup Recipe

Preparation time: 10 minutes

Cooking Time: 10 minutes

Serving: 4

Ingredients:

- Soy sauce, two tablespoon

- Chopped garlic, two teaspoon
- Green onions, three tablespoon
- Tempeh, two cups
- Chopped onions, one cup
- Asian sesame oil, one tablespoon
- Vegetable oil, two tablespoon
- Salt to taste
- Black pepper to taste
- Vegetable broth, three cups
- Cilantro, one tablespoon
- Coconut milk, one cup

Instructions:
1. Warm a wok.
2. Add about a tablespoon of oil.
3. Add the onions
4. Fry them, and then add garlic.
5. Add the tempeh and mix.
6. Add the coconut milk.
7. Add somewhat more oil if you need it and mix.
8. Add about a teaspoon of soy sauce to the wok.
9. Add in the salt and pepper.
10. Add the vegetable broth into the wok.
11. Let it cook until a thick curry forms.
12. Garnish with cilantro and green onions.
13. Plate and serve quickly.

3.18 Thai Vegan Quinoa Crunch Salad Recipe

Preparation time: 25 minutes

Cooking Time: 5 minutes

Serving: 4

Ingredients:

- Asian Sesame oil, two tablespoon
- Chopped garlic, two teaspoon
- Green onions, three tablespoon
- Edamame, two cups
- Cooked quinoa, two cups
- Cooked peas, one cup
- Broccoli, one cup
- Red cabbage, one cup
- Avocados, two
- Thai creamy dressing, two tablespoon
- Soy sauce, two tablespoon
- Salt to taste
- Black pepper to taste
- Peanuts, two cups
- Lime juice, two tablespoon

Instructions:

1. Cut all the things in the same way.
2. Add in all the ingredients in a bowl.

3. Mix the ingredients well and add more dressing if you like.

4. Your dish is ready to be served.

3.19 Thai Green Papaya Salad Recipe

Preparation time: 25 minutes

Cooking Time: 5 minutes

Serving: 4

Ingredients:

- Asian Sesame oil, two tablespoon
- Chopped garlic, two teaspoon
- Green onions, three tablespoon
- Edamame, two cups
- Papaya, two cups
- Cooked peas, one cup
- Crotons, one cup
- Red cabbage, one cup
- Avocados, two
- Thai green dressing, two tablespoon
- Soy sauce, two tablespoon
- Salt to taste
- Black pepper to taste
- Peanuts, two cups
- Lime juice, two tablespoon

Instructions:

1. Cut all the things in the same way.
2. Add in all the ingredients in a bowl.
3. Mix the ingredients well and add more dressing if you like.
4. Your dish is ready to be served.

3.20 Thai Coconut Chickpea Curry Recipe

Preparation time: 10 minutes

Cooking Time: 10 minutes

Serving: 4

Ingredients:

- Soy sauce, two tablespoon
- Chopped garlic, two teaspoon
- Green onions, three tablespoon
- Chickpeas, two cups
- Chopped onions, one cup
- Asian sesame oil, one tablespoon
- Vegetable oil, two tablespoon
- Salt to taste
- Black pepper to taste
- Fish sauce, two tablespoon
- Vegetable broth, three cups
- Cilantro, one tablespoon
- Coconut milk, one cup
- Crushed coconut flakes, half cup

Instructions:

1. Warm a wok.
2. Add about a tablespoon of oil.
3. Add the onions
4. Fry them, and then add garlic.
5. Add the chickpeas and mix.
6. Add the coconut milk.
7. Add somewhat more oil if you need it and mix.
8. Add about a teaspoon of soy sauce and fish sauce to the wok.
9. Add in the salt and pepper.
10. Add the vegetable broth into the wok.
11. Add in the shredded coconut flakes.
12. Let it cook until a thick curry forms.
13. Garnish with cilantro and green onions.
14. Plate and serve quickly.

Chapter 4: Veggie Thai Snack Recipes

In this chapter you will learn some amazing wok vegetarian snack dishes that you can easy make at home on your own.

4.1 Thai Vegan Almond Pad Thai Sauce Recipe

Preparation time: 25 minutes

Cooking Time: 15 minutes

Serving: 4

Ingredients:

- Asian Sesame oil, two tablespoon
- Chopped garlic, two teaspoon
- Green onions, three tablespoon
- Sugar, half cup
- Almonds, two cups
- Chopped fresh dill, two tablespoon
- Vegetable oil, two tablespoon
- Salt to taste
- Black pepper to taste
- Melon seeds, half cup
- Chopped onions, one cup

Instructions:

1. Heat a wok.

2. Add in all the ingredients except the melon seeds, sugar, and almonds.

3. Once the mixture is cooked, add in the almonds and melon seeds and cook them until they are tender.

4. In a separate wok, add in the sugar and let it melt.

5. Once caramelized, add it into the melon seeds and almonds mixture.

6. Grind the mixture.

7. Your dip is ready to be served.

4.2 Thai Vegan Roasted Cauliflower Pizza Recipe

Preparation time: 25 minutes

Cooking Time: 25 minutes

Serving: 4

Ingredients:

- Asian Sesame oil, two tablespoon
- Chopped garlic, two teaspoon
- Green onions, three tablespoon
- Bell pepper strips, half cup
- Pizza dough, one pack
- Chopped fresh dill, two tablespoon
- Vegetable oil, two tablespoon
- Soy sauce, two tablespoon
- Fish sauce, two tablespoon
- Salt to taste

- BBQ sauce, half cup
- Black pepper to taste
- Ginger paste, two teaspoon
- Cauliflower florets, two cups
- Mixed cheese, one cup
- Chopped onions, two tablespoon
- Olives, half cup
- Thai dried basil, half teaspoon
- Thai dried oregano, half teaspoon

Instructions:

1. Firstly prepare the cauliflower mixture.
2. In a pan, heat the vegetable oil.
3. When the oil is heated properly, add in the onions.
4. When the onions turn translucent, add in the garlic and ginger.
5. Let the onions, ginger, and garlic cook for two to three minutes.
6. Add in the vegetables.
7. Let the vegetables stir fry.
8. Add in the soy and fish sauce.
9. Add in the salt and pepper.
10. Once the mixture is ready, remove it from the stove.
11. Knead the dough and roll it out in the form of pizza bread in a round structure.

12. Lay the bread on a baking dish.

13. Add the sesame oil on top.

14. Add the bbq sauce on top of the bread and evenly spread the sauce all over.

15. Add the vegetable mixture on top of the bread.

16. Add the olives and the dried oregano as well as basil leaves.

17. Add the cheese on top of all.

18. Place your pizza in the oven for twenty five minutes.

19. Once the cheese melts and the dough turn golden brown, switch off the oven.

20. Your dish is ready to be served.

4.3 Vegan Thai Corn Fritters Recipe

Preparation time: 25 minutes

Cooking Time: 15 minutes

Serving: 4

Ingredients:

- Chopped garlic, two teaspoon
- Green onions, three tablespoon
- Cooked corn, two cups
- Chopped fresh dill, two tablespoon
- Vegetable oil, as required
- Cumin spice, two tablespoon
- Salt to taste
- Gram flour, two cups

- Chopped onions, two tablespoon
- Water, as required

Instructions:

1. Mix all the ingredients.
2. Heat the oil in a large pan.
3. Make small fritters and fry them.
4. When the fritters are golden brown, dish them out.
5. Serve them with your preferred dip.
6. Your dish is ready to be served.

4.4 Thai Sweet Potatoes and Cauliflower Lettuce Wrap Recipe

Preparation time: 25 minutes

Cooking Time: 25 minutes

Serving: 4

Ingredients:

- Asian Sesame oil, two tablespoon
- Chopped garlic, two teaspoon
- Green onions, three tablespoon
- Tortilla sheets, one
- Chopped fresh dill, two tablespoon
- Vegetable oil, two tablespoon
- Soy sauce, two tablespoon

- Fish sauce, two tablespoon
- Salt to taste
- Black pepper to taste
- Ginger paste, two teaspoon
- Cauliflower florets, two cups
- Sweet potatoes, one cup
- Chopped onions, two tablespoon
- Olives, half cup
- Thai dried basil, half teaspoon
- Thai dried oregano, half teaspoon

Instructions:

1. Firstly prepare the cauliflower mixture.
2. In a pan, heat the vegetable oil.
3. When the oil is heated properly, add in the onions.
4. When the onions turn translucent, add in the garlic and ginger.
5. Let the onions, ginger, and garlic cook for two to three minutes.
6. Add in the vegetables.
7. Let the vegetables stir fry.
8. Add in the soy and fish sauce.
9. Add in the salt and pepper.

10. Once the mixture is ready, remove it from the stove.

11. Lay the lettuce leaves.

12. Add the sesame oil on top.

13. Add the vegetable mixture on top of the lettuce.

14. Add the olives and the dried oregano as well as basil leaves.

15. Wrap your lettuce leaves.

16. Your dish is ready to be served.

4.5 Thai Vegan Curry Tacos Recipe

Preparation time: 10 minutes

Cooking Time: 10 minutes

Serving: 4

Ingredients:

- Soy sauce, two tablespoon
- Chopped garlic, two teaspoon
- Green onions, three tablespoon
- Mix vegetables, two cups
- Chopped onions, one cup
- Asian sesame oil, one tablespoon
- Taco shells, eight
- Thai curry paste, two tablespoon
- Vegetable oil, two tablespoon
- Salt to taste
- Black pepper to taste

- Vegetable broth, two cups
- Cilantro, one tablespoon

Instructions:

1. Warm a wok.
2. Add about a tablespoon of oil.
3. Add the onions
4. Fry them, and then add garlic.
5. Add the vegetables and mix.
6. Add somewhat more oil if you need it and mix.
7. Add about a teaspoon of curry paste, soy sauce to the wok.
8. Add in the salt and pepper.
9. Add the vegetable broth into the wok.
10. Let it cook until a thick curry forms.
11. Heat the taco shells.
12. Add the formed mixture into the taco shells.
13. Garnish with cilantro and green onions.
14. Plate and serve quickly.

4.6 Thai Peanut Cauliflower Fritters Recipe

Preparation time: 25 minutes

Cooking Time: 15 minutes

Serving: 4

Ingredients:

- Chopped garlic, two teaspoon
- Green onions, three tablespoon
- Peanuts, two cups
- Chopped fresh dill, two tablespoon
- Vegetable oil, as required
- Cumin spice, two tablespoon
- Salt to taste
- Gram flour, two cups
- Chopped onions, two tablespoon
- Cauliflower florets, one cup
- Water, as required

Instructions:

7. Mix all the ingredients.
8. Heat the oil in a large pan.
9. Make small fritters and fry them.
10. When the fritters are golden brown, dish them out.
11. Serve them with your preferred dip.
12. Your dish is ready to be served.

4.7 Thai Fried Tempeh Recipe

Preparation time: 25 minutes

Cooking Time: 15 minutes

Serving: 4

Ingredients:

- Asian Sesame oil, two tablespoon
- Chopped garlic, two teaspoon
- Green onions, three tablespoon
- Tempeh, two cups
- Chopped fresh dill, two tablespoon
- Vegetable oil, two tablespoon
- Soy sauce, two tablespoon
- Salt to taste
- Black pepper to taste
- Mix Thai spice, one tablespoon
- Chopped onions, two tablespoon

Instructions:

1. Heat a pan.
2. Add the vegetable oil and then add the onions.
3. When onions are almost done, add in the garlic.
4. Add the tempeh cubes.
5. Fry the tempeh cubes along with the garlic and onion.
6. When the tempeh is done, add in the rest of the ingredients.
7. Cook the tempeh along with the spices, and make sure to not burn your dish.
8. Add a few drops of water after a few seconds.

9. Garnish your dish with cilantro and fresh chopped dill.

10.   Your dish is ready to be served.

4.8 Thai Sweet Potato Skins Recipe

Preparation time: 25 minutes

Cooking Time: 15 minutes

Serving: 4

Ingredients:

- Asian Sesame oil, two tablespoon
- Chopped garlic, two teaspoon
- Green onions, three tablespoon
- Mozzarella cheese, half cup
- Mixed vegetables, two cups
- Chopped fresh dill, two tablespoon
- Vegetable oil, two tablespoon
- Soy sauce, two tablespoon
- Salt to taste
- Black pepper to taste
- Sweet potatoes, two cups
- Chopped onions, two tablespoon

Instructions:

1. In a bowl, mix the mozzarella cheese, mixed vegetables, chopped garlic, green onions, salt,

pepper, chopped onions, soy sauce, fresh dill, and sesame oil.

2. Remove the inner sides of the sweet potatoes.

3. Add the above-formed mixture into the sweet potatoes filling it.

4. In a large wok, place these filled sweet potatoes.

5. Spray non-stick cooking spray.

6. Cover the wok and let it cook for ten minutes.

7. Your dish is ready to be served.

4.9 Thai Pumpkin Hummus Recipe

Preparation time: 25 minutes

Cooking Time: 15 minutes

Serving: 4

Ingredients:

- Asian Sesame oil, two tablespoon
- Chopped garlic, two teaspoon
- Green onions, three tablespoon
- Olive oil, half cup
- Hard boiled chickpeas, two cups
- Chopped fresh dill, two tablespoon
- Fish sauce, two tablespoon
- Soy sauce, two tablespoon
- Salt to taste
- Black pepper to taste
- Pumpkin, two cups
- Chopped onions, two tablespoon

Instructions:

1. Boil your chickpeas but do not over boil it, so it does not turn too soft.

2. Add the pumpkin and also boil it for five minutes or until it turns a little soft.

3. Place all the ingredients in a blender.

4. Blend all your mixture.

5. You can garnish your hummus with a little cilantro leaf if you like.

6. Your pumpkin hummus is ready to be served.

4.10 Thai Vegan Eggplant Dip Recipe

Preparation time: 25 minutes

Cooking Time: 15 minutes

Serving: 4

Ingredients:

- Asian Sesame oil, two tablespoon
- Chopped garlic, two teaspoon
- Green onions, three tablespoon
- Olive oil, half cup
- Eggplant, two cups
- Chopped fresh dill, two tablespoon
- Fish sauce, two tablespoon
- Soy sauce, two tablespoon
- Salt to taste

- Black pepper to taste
- Shredded coconut flakes, half cup
- Chopped onions, two tablespoon

Instructions:

1. Add the eggplant and boil it for five minutes or until it turns a little soft.
2. Place all the ingredients in a blender.
3. Blend all your mixture.
4. You can garnish your dip with a little cilantro leaf if you like.
5. Your pumpkin dip is ready to be served.

4.11 Thai Vegan Sandwiches Recipe

Preparation time: 25 minutes

Cooking Time: 15 minutes

Serving: 4

Ingredients:

- Asian Sesame oil, two tablespoon
- Chopped garlic, two teaspoon
- Green onions, three tablespoon
- Bell pepper strips, half cup
- Carrots, two cups
- Lettuce as required
- Bread slices, eight
- Chopped fresh dill, two tablespoon

- Butter, two tablespoon
- Soy spread, two tablespoon
- Salt to taste
- Black pepper to taste
- Mushrooms, two cups
- Eggs, six
- Chopped onions, two tablespoon

Instructions:

1. Assemble your sandwiches.
2. Add all the ingredients into the bread slices and then toast your sandwiches with the help of butter.
3. Your sandwiches will turn golden brown on both sides.
4. You can serve your sandwiches with any dip or sauce you like.

4.12 Thai Mango Coleslaw Recipe

Preparation time: 25 minutes

Cooking Time: 5 minutes

Serving: 4

Ingredients:

- Asian Sesame oil, two tablespoon
- Chopped garlic, two teaspoon
- Green onions, three tablespoon

- Green mango, two cups
- Carrots, two cups
- Corn, one cup
- Green cabbage, one cup
- Red cabbage, one cup
- Avocados, two
- Thai creamy dressing, two tablespoon
- Soy sauce, two tablespoon
- Salt to taste
- Black pepper to taste
- Lime juice, two tablespoon
- Coconut flakes, half cu

Instructions:

1. Cut all the things in the same way.
2. Add in all the ingredients in a bowl.
3. Mix the ingredients well and add more dressing if you like.
4. Your dish is ready to be served.

4.13 Thai Green Curry Guacamole Recipe

Preparation time: 25 minutes

Cooking Time: 15 minutes

Serving: 4

Ingredients:

- Asian Sesame oil, two tablespoon

- Chopped garlic, two teaspoon
- Green onions, three tablespoon
- Olive oil, half cup
- Green curry paste, two tablespoon
- Chopped fresh dill, two tablespoon
- Fish sauce, two tablespoon
- Soy sauce, two tablespoon
- Salt to taste
- Black pepper to taste
- Avocados, two cups
- Chopped onions, two tablespoon

Instructions:

1. Cut the avocados into pieces.
2. Place all the ingredients in a blender.
3. Blend all your mixture.
4. You can garnish your guacamole with a little cilantro leaf if you like.
5. Your pumpkin guacamole is ready to be served.

4.14 Thai Coconut Custard Dip Recipe

Preparation time: 25 minutes

Cooking Time: 15 minutes

Serving: 4

Ingredients:

- Asian Sesame oil, two tablespoon

- Chopped garlic, two teaspoon
- Green onions, three tablespoon
- Olive oil, half cup
- Coconut pieces, two cups
- Chopped fresh dill, two tablespoon
- Fish sauce, two tablespoon
- Soy sauce, two tablespoon
- Salt to taste
- Black pepper to taste
- Vanilla Custard, two cups
- Shredded coconut flakes, half cup
- Chopped onions, two tablespoon

Instructions:

1. Add the coconut pieces and boil it for five minutes or until it turns a little soft.
2. Place all the ingredients in a blender.
3. Blend all your mixture.
4. You can garnish your hummus with shredded coconut flakes if you like.
5. Your pumpkin hummus is ready to be served.

4.15 Thai Vegan Rolls Recipe

Preparation time: 25 minutes

Cooking Time: 15 minutes

Serving: 4

Ingredients:

- Asian Sesame oil, two tablespoon
- Chopped garlic, two teaspoon
- Green onions, three tablespoon
- Mix vegetables, half cup
- Chopped fresh dill, two tablespoon
- Vegetable oil, as required
- Soy sauce, to serve
- Salt to taste
- Black pepper to taste
- Avocado cubes, one cup
- Wonton wraps, as required
- Water, as required

Instructions:

1. In a wok, add one tablespoon of oil.
2. Add in the mixed vegetables and cook for two minutes.
3. Add salt and pepper.
4. When cooked, add the mixture into a bowl.
5. Mix in the avocado cubes with the mixture.
6. Add the prepared mixture into the wonton wrappers and fold them into a roll.
7. Fry the rolls in a small amount of oil in the wok.
8. Serve your vegan rolls with soy sauce or any other sauce that you may prefer.

4.16 Broccoli Fritters Recipe

Preparation time: 25 minutes

Cooking Time: 15 minutes

Serving: 4

Ingredients:

- Chopped garlic, two teaspoon
- Green onions, three tablespoon
- Broccoli, two cups
- Chopped fresh dill, two tablespoon
- Vegetable oil, as required
- Cumin spice, two tablespoon
- Salt to taste
- Gram flour, two cups
- Chopped onions, two tablespoon
- Water, as required

Instructions:

1. Mix all the ingredients.
2. Heat the oil in a large pan.
3. Make small fritters and fry them.
4. When the fritters are golden brown, dish them out.
5. Serve them with your preferred dip.
6. Your dish is ready to be served.

4.17 Thai Quinoa Bombs Recipe

Preparation time: 25 minutes

Cooking Time: 20 minutes

Serving: 4-6

Ingredients:

- Quinoa mixture, two cup
- Bread dough, two cups
- Salt to taste
- Egg wash, one

Instructions:

1. Knead the dough until it becomes soft and fluffly.
2. One dough is done it is time to make small pieces out of the dough.
3. Place your quinoa mixture on the dough and shape it into round balls.
4. Cover each ball with egg wash and bake for fifteen minutes.
5. Your dish is ready to be served.

4.18 Thai Peanut Hummus Recipe

Preparation time: 25 minutes

Cooking Time: 15 minutes

Serving: 4

Ingredients:

- Asian Sesame oil, two tablespoon
- Chopped garlic, two teaspoon
- Green onions, three tablespoon
- Olive oil, half cup
- Hard boiled chickpeas, two cups
- Chopped fresh dill, two tablespoon
- Fish sauce, two tablespoon
- Soy sauce, two tablespoon
- Salt to taste
- Black pepper to taste
- Peanuts, two cups
- Chopped onions, two tablespoon

Instructions:

1. Place all the ingredients in a blender.
2. Blend all your mixture.
3. You can garnish your hummus with a little cilantro leaf if you like.
4. Your peanut hummus is ready to be served.

4.19 Thai Spicy Peanut Dip Recipe

Preparation time: 25 minutes

Cooking Time: 15 minutes

Serving: 4

Ingredients:

- Asian Sesame oil, two tablespoon
- Chopped garlic, two teaspoon
- Green onions, three tablespoon
- Olive oil, half cup
- Peanuts, two cups
- Chopped fresh dill, two tablespoon
- Fish sauce, two tablespoon
- Soy sauce, two tablespoon
- Salt to taste
- Black pepper to taste
- Chili paste, two tablespoon

Instructions:
1. Blend all your mixture.
2. You can garnish your dip with a little cilantro leaf if you like.
3. Your dip is ready to be served.

4.20 Thai Bean Spread Recipe

Preparation time: 25 minutes

Cooking Time: 15 minutes

Serving: 4

Ingredients:
- Asian Sesame oil, two tablespoon

- Chopped garlic, two teaspoon
- Green onions, three tablespoon
- Olive oil, half cup
- Black beans, two cups
- Chopped fresh dill, two tablespoon
- Fish sauce, two tablespoon
- Soy sauce, two tablespoon
- Salt to taste
- Black pepper to taste
- While beans, two cups
- Chopped onions, two tablespoon

Instructions:

1. Place all the ingredients in a blender.
2. Blend all your mixture.
3. You can garnish your spread with cilantro leaves if you like.
4. Your spread is ready to be served.

Conclusion

While carrying on with bustling life, food turns into the solitary wellspring of satisfaction for people in the 21st century. Various foods are accessible on the planet, and everyone is entirely unexpected from the other. Thai cooking covers dishes from Thailand, and Thai nourishments are incredibly well known in the U.S.A.

The different flavors utilized in Thai cooking have a tremendous measure of astounding properties that soundly affects our general wellbeing. This cookbook incorporates healthy plans that contain breakfast, lunch, dinner, and snack recipes that you can undoubtedly make at home without the help of any kind. Anyway, why order or go out for Thai food when you can be the Thai culinary expert at your home? Start reading and start cooking with this amazing and easy cookbook.

Printed in Great Britain
by Amazon

14482906R00061